95-YEAR-OLD PARROTS!

By Leonard Atlantic

Gareth Stevens
PUBLISHING

Please visit our website, www.garethstevens.com. For a free color catalog of all our high-quality books, call toll free 1-800-542-2595 or fax 1-877-542-2596.

Cataloging-in-Publication Data

Names: Atlantic, Leonard.
Title: 95-year-old parrots! / Leonard Atlantic.
Description: New York : Gareth Stevens Publishing, 2017. | Series: World's longest-living animals | Includes index.
Identifiers: ISBN 9781482456165 (pbk.) | ISBN 9781482456189 (library bound) | ISBN 9781482456172 (6 pack)
Subjects: LCSH: Parrots–Juvenile literature.
Classification: LCC QL696.P7 A43 2017 | DDC 598.7'1–dc23

Published in 2017 by
Gareth Stevens Publishing
111 East 14th Street, Suite 349
New York, NY 10003

Designer: Andrea Davison-Bartolotta and Bethany Perl
Editor: Ryan Nagelhout

Photo credits: Cover, p. 1 LifetimeStock/Shutterstock.com; pp. 2–24 (background) Dmitrieva Olga/Shutterstock.com; p. 5 (Amazon) aabeele/Shutterstock.com; p. 5 (Kakapoo) FunkMonk/Wikipedia.org; p. 5 (macaw) Junior Braz/Shutterstock.com; p. 7 bikeriderlondon/Shutterstock.com; p. 9 Tracy Starr/Shutterstock.com; p. 11 (cockatoo) Rosa Jay/Shutterstock.com; p. 11 (parrot) Zoltan Major/Shutterstock.com; p. 13 Andreas Krone/Shutterstock.com; p. 15 Meaning/Shutterstock.com; p. 17 Kakapo Sirocco/Wikipedia.org; p. 19 apiguide/Shutterstock.com; p. 21 (parrot) JJ Harrison/Wikipedia.org; p. 21 (macaw) Jeff Kubina/Wikipedia.org.

Printed in the United States of America

CPSIA compliance information: Batch #CW17GS: For further information contact Gareth Stevens, New York, New York at 1-800-542-2595.

CONTENTS

Boldface words appear in the glossary.

Kinds of Parrots

There are more than 350 different kinds of parrots. Macaws, parakeets, and Amazons are all brightly colored kinds of parrots. Some of these amazing animals can live a very long time—and kakapos (KAH-kuh-pohs) can live up to 95 years!

MACAW

AMAZON

KAKAPO

Beaks and Eats

All parrots have a curved mouthpart called a beak. Their beak helps them eat lots of different foods. Parrots are omnivores. This means they eat both plants and animals. They love eating fruit, seeds, nuts, flowers, and even some bugs.

Count the Toes!

Parrots live in warm places all over the world. All parrots have four toes on each foot. Two toes point forward, and two toes point backward. These toes help them grab onto branches of trees where they live.

TOES ➡

Big and Small

Parrots come in many sizes. The smallest are **pygmy** parrots. They are just 3.5 inches (8.9 cm) tall and weigh 2.25 ounces (63.8 g). Large parrots like macaws and cockatoos can grow to 40 inches (100 cm) and weigh 3.5 pounds (1.6 kg)!

COCKATOO

40 in.

11

PYGMY PARROT

3.5 in.

Talk Back

People like parrots because they're colorful and smart. Some, such as the African gray parrot, can even **mimic** human speech! Parrots don't understand what they're saying—they're just copying the words they hear people say.

AFRICAN GRAY
PARROT

13

Pet Birds

In the wild, parrots can live up to 80 years. But many live longer when kept as pets. Macaws, cockatiels, parakeets, and cockatoos are often kept as pets. Parrots in zoos live a long time in **captivity**, too.

Kakapos

Kakapos are some of the weirdest and oldest parrots. They live in New Zealand. They're the only parrots in the world that can't fly! They're also **nocturnal**. Some people think kakapos can live up to 95 years!

Poncho

One of the oldest and most famous parrots is a movie star! Poncho is a green-winged macaw. She was 75 years old when she was featured in *102 Dalmatians* in 2000. The parrot **retired** from acting after the movie, but **celebrated** her 90th birthday in 2015!

GREEN-WINGED MACAW

Keeping Them Alive

Some parrots, such as the orange-bellied parrot and the blue-throated macaw, are **endangered**. Other parrots are taken away from their homes in the wild to become pets. If parrots are to keep living amazingly long lives, people need to keep them safe.

BLUE-THROATED MACAW

ORANGE-BELLIED PARROT

GLOSSARY

captivity: the state or condition of being kept caged

celebrate: to honor with special activities

endangered: in danger of dying out

mimic: to copy

nocturnal: active at night

pygmy: an animal very small for its kind

retire: to leave a job

FOR MORE INFORMATION

BOOKS

Bowman, Chris. *Parrots*. Minneapolis, MN: Bellwether Media, 2015.

Hand, Carol. *12 Super-Smart Animals You Need to Know*. North Mankato, MN: 12-Story Library, 2016.

WEBSITES

Parrot

animals.nationalgeographic.com/animals/birds/parrot/

Learn more about where parrots live here.

Parrots

animals.sandiegozoo.org/animals/parrot

Learn about different sizes of parrots on this site.

INDEX